ADVANCE PRAISE

With abundant joy and enthusiasm, Kimberlie Chenoweth demonstrates both her mastery and the embodiment of what she teaches in her beautiful second book—that as women, we are waking up to our role in the evolution of consciousness, and that we're called to do some healing on behalf of the world—as she literally "walks earth-anchored wholeness into her bones" with and for us. Don't miss the richness of *Walking in Wholeness*. It is a knockout!

Anne Hillman, Author, *Awakening the Energies of Love,* 2nd Edition, *and The Dancing Animal Woman*

Kimberlie Chenoweth is a clear golden voice in a world that has filled itself with noise. Her message to women in all walks of life is precisely what we need to reorganize our world for renewed generativity, true wholeness, and creative fulfillment. She delivers a message that is at once immediate for the individual and global for modern culture. So if you're seeking a way to blossom yourself, and have the courage to discover how much you matter in this world, read this book and seek out Kimberlie.

Marti Spiegelman, *Founder: Shamans Light™ Indigenous initiation and mentoring for your genius; and Awakening Value™: Technologies of Consciousness for Thriving in Business*

Wow! What a fresh perspective on the age-old problem of how to live a fulfilling life in stressful times. *Walking in Wholeness* is a brilliant and masterful work of art. It brings key indigenous principles of consciousness (as known and lived in the Andes) to life in the Western world in a very relatable and practical way. Kimberlie has initiated a movement, showing us how to begin weaving the principle of original wholeness back into our busy lives and the communities to which we belong. I have nothing but deep respect and honor for Kimberlie's beautiful wisdom voice collectively spoken into the world.

Ellen Bachmeyer, LCSW, Founder, The Windhorse Center

I love this book: *Walking in Wholeness.* It reminds us about the importance of calling forth our forgotten dreams, many of which have been dormant since childhood. I love how Kimberlie invites us all to remember—and to once again—experience the beautiful and sacred gifts that come from our connection with Mother Earth. I love how *Walking in Wholeness*, gently encourages and shows us a truer path: one that is often found right beneath our feet; one that can lead us toward our authentic selves where our joys, hopes, needs, dreams and visions are seen, heard, validated and given wings to soar.

Jacquelyn Strickland, Licensed Professional Counselor, HSP; Co-Founder, with Dr. Elaine Aron, of the HSP (Highly Sensitive People) Gathering Retreats Since 2001

Ancient wisdom finds new expression for these modern times through this beautifully crafted book, *Walking in Wholeness*. The chapters reveal basic truths that are woven into an intricate web, inviting women (and men) to grow as unique individuals, finding their authentic voices, and discovering true collectivity. The invitation is to remember this web of living systems in which we each play an important role, and Kimberlie awakens the place from which to begin.

Suza Bedient, Founder, Tree of Life Mentoring

In *Walking in Wholeness*, Kimberlie Chenoweth extends a wonderful invitation to women for their dreams to blossom. She intimately captures what it is like for women to feel trapped in a life of forgotten dreams, and then offers a hopeful and truly inspiring pathway to the fulfillment of wholeness. Along the way her down to earth examples provide a credibility that becomes real permission for women to take action and reclaim the authenticity they had lost or left behind.

P.S. While this book is designed for women, Kimberlie's insights into the integration of the feminine and masculine in each of us opens the door for men to joyfully absorb her wisdom just as well.

Tim Bachmeyer, Ph.D., President, the Andean Research Institute

Somewhere along the way, we lost our way as women. We came to believe that we should place all of our needs, dreams and desires on the back burner in order to help our children, our families and those we love. We were taught to believe that tending to our own needs and desires is selfish, but it is only when we tend to our own well-being that we have anything of value to give to anyone else.

Kimberlie Chenoweth will challenge the way you think about wholeness; rather than seeing it as a theoretical concept, she moves it into an active way of being in the world for women everywhere. This is your guidebook for discovering and aligning to your life's purpose.

Sharon Pope, Master Life Coach and International Best Selling Author of the *Soulful Truth Telling Series*

Walking in WHOLENESS

Women Reclaiming Authentic Passion, Purpose, and Power

KIMBERLIE CHENOWETH

COPYRIGHT

DISCLAIMER

Cover Design: Heidi Miller
Editing: Kate Makled
Author's photo courtesy of Kelley Cox

DEDICATION

For Amy, Hollis, Jodi,
Leslie and Tori

– and –

For Shams,
emissary of unconditional love,
freedom, and joy

TABLE OF
CONTENTS

INTRODUCTION

We delight in the beauty of the butterfly, but rarely admit the changes it has gone through to achieve that beauty. MAYA ANGELOU

It's no secret the world is changing. All over the planet, women are waking up to our roles as stewards and co-creators of a better world for all. We're striving to embrace and embody our value, and the power to heal and change. We get that our very being is vital to the well-being of the planet, which means that our own well-being must also be stewarded. We dream of flowing blessings of love and light to our communities, joining hearts in mutual celebration of one another's power and beauty, but with everything else on our plates those moments in reality are fleeting at best. With all the other obligations in our lives, it seems we have to work extra hard to carve out time for our dreams.

We have some trailblazers—visionary women such as Marianne Williamson, Maya Angelou, Terry Tempest Williams, and Malala—who are beacons of light inspiring us to our best selves. These are four powerful, contemporary women, the kind of role models we seek to lead the way today. They are women of courage and powerful voice. Women around whom other women gather to remember their own truth and power, and what it means to be a woman in the Western world. Women who have started movements with truth at the core of their messages. Of love. Of healing. Of education for all. Women who inspire other women to also be leaders.

These are four powerful women who embody *wholeness* in new and creative ways, beyond past definitions and maybe even beyond definition itself. In this book, you'll have an opportunity to consider wholeness in a new way, too—as more than a longed-for goal you hope to one day, finally, achieve. For our purposes here, wholeness is really more of a verb—an active way of being in the world, around which to organize any and every activity in our busy lives. In the original, indigenous understanding, wholeness starts with a big, beautiful taproot in the land that provides a way to thrive, and even to flourish. This understanding of wholeness reveals a surprisingly uncomplicated way to show up with both the challenges and joys of life as we grow, create, and align with our soul's sense of mission and purpose.

I have a dream that women come together in dynamic communities to reclaim the purposes they're here to serve, the happiness they deserve, and the tribes to which they belong.

I have a dream that we heed the call to bring forward our wisdom to heal and change the world.

I have a dream that visionary women may step forward in wholeness, as models of possibility for those who have forgotten.

This book is a call to women to walk—together—into a world of well-being and wholeness.

Perhaps this dream seems impractical, especially given how busy, stressed out, driven, isolated, or lost many women are feeling. We have a long way to go, but I believe it is entirely within our reach to realize. Maybe not in our lifetime, but perhaps for our children or grandchildren to succeed if we start the movement and the momentum now.

We can't make the needed changes alone. We need each other. We need mentors and guides. As women, we require transformative time alone, yes, but we also need our tribes.

This book is a call to join communities where we are able to remember and apply the wisdom of the "old indigenous soul" residing in our very bones—a way of walking in wholeness that transcends time, busyness, all the stressors of our daily lives, and even the thought that we can or should figure things out on our own. The way forward is collective.

Indigenous cultures around the world have a lot to teach us about the way forward. The knowledge of wholeness we'll be exploring is grounded in the timeless wisdom of a long lineage of Andean medicine people. They are masters of the energy of love, light, and wholeness. They know how to land spiritual truths in the here and now, and they know this knowledge is meant to be shared with the world. They are urging us to take it and apply it in modern, Western culture. For these teachers, wholeness is an organizing principle around which we're all meant to live and thrive. As an organizing principle, wholeness is equally available to each of us as we strive to create well-being for ourselves, our loved ones, and the communities to which we belong.

Most of the work I do is with women, helping them to consciously remember and engage their capacity to create meaningful lives through the lens of wholeness. This book will reveal and explore the interwoven magic of wholeness and community in ways that I hope you'll be able to tap into and use for yourself. We'll take a look, chapter by chapter, at what it means to walk together in wholeness as women in today's world.

We'll start in Chapter One, "The Challenge," a discussion of some of the core challenges women face in today's world. Each of the subsequent chapters includes a bit of material addressed in other chapters, because there are places in the discussion that one energy can't be disconnected from the other and still convey the full meaning. Ultimately, they all come together to form a coherent whole.

Chapter Two, "Why Wholeness?" shares how I came to the understanding of wholeness unfolded here, and offers a first glimpse into what wholeness really means. Chapter Three, "Why Women?" talks about why we have been called to lead the way as healers and change-makers in the world. Chapter Four explores "Why Walking?"—an allusion to the importance of dynamic expression in the world. Chapter Five, "Why Community?" introduces a beautiful experience of belonging and making a difference that's completely possible, even in our busy lives today. And finally Chapter Six, "Commencement" will bring all these elements together in chorus for restoring wholeness.

CHAPTER ONE

The Challenge

I did not know I was on a search for passionate aliveness. I only knew I was lonely and lost and that something was drawing me deeper beneath the surface of my life in search of meaning....

It is a yearning to be all that we can be.

ANNE HILLMAN, THE DANCING ANIMAL WOMAN

Visionary women. We have big dreams (or at least we used to.) Many of us grew up hoping to change the world, that we would be able to actualize ourselves as we grew into contributors and maybe leaders. We believed we could become whatever we could imagine. For many women, today those dreams feel far away, consumed by the many other demands on our time and energy.

Some days it seems impossible that we will ever be able to make whatever fundamental changes are needed in order to simplify the demands on our time. We get caught up in activities and entire lives that don't reflect the vision we've held of what's possible. We're overly busy with jobs, marriages, children, the stuff of daily scheduling, to such an extent there's little time or space for our own dreams.

We long for a simpler life, a more complete life. We long for time to work on our own projects, no matter how modest or grand. We long to speak up and show up. Some of us regularly feel trapped, so burdened by the responsibilities we've taken on and commitments we've made that it seems there may be no way out.

But the yearning is still there, showing up as a big "something" inside that cries out for expression in the world.

I remember clearly the day that Jennifer commented to the other women in one of my mentoring groups, "The life I'm living doesn't look like the life I imagined for myself." She had been in a process of remembering her big, lifelong dreams, and was registering the discrepancy between those dreams and the structured reality of her current lifestyle.

Everyone nodded in agreement.

I was stunned at the resonance generated by this simple statement.

How can it possibly be okay for so many women to be living a reality that doesn't match up to what they have dreamed possible for themselves?

Your biggest life dreams reveal important aspects of your identity and purpose. But without time and energy to pursue your dreams, they fade to background. When you don't have ample opportunity to move toward realizing your dreams, you might end up believing them to be ultimately unimportant, unachievable, or childish fantasy, or even regarding yourself as unworthy or incapable.

Let's look at some of the factors contributing to this common problem.

We're too busy

Nearly every woman I know faces every day with a busy schedule and a feeling they're doing more than they want to be doing, or even should be doing. Whether it's work responsibilities, caring for aging parents, raising a family, or other obligations, big dreams get lost in the demands of meeting everyday expectations.

Expert as we are at tracking and meeting the needs of others, it can be challenging at best to focus, uninterrupted, on any particular project of our own. Even reading a book can be fraught with multiple interruptions per page, say nothing for the daunting task of carving out sacred time to write your *own* book, return to the canvas to paint, take on that creative idea you had for a part time business, or go for a hike.

While this can be true in any season of adult life, I want to share with you the story of a woman in her early 40's.

When Lindsey first reached out to me, she said, "I used to have a life—things I loved to do, projects I believed in, a close circle of girlfriends. Dreams. Now I spend most my time checking things off my to-do list and taking care of other people—my kids, my husband, my boss. I love my family, and I want them all to have what they need. But Steven and I rarely get the chance to connect with each other without the kids around. And after working five mornings a week, chasing kids all afternoon, buying groceries, trying to keep up with the house, and finally getting the boys to bed, I'm stressed out, exhausted, and edgy. All I can do is crash with a glass of wine in front of the TV, pushing the 'like' button on my friends' Facebook posts and sharing funny cat videos. I feel completely lost in the to-do list of life. I never get to recharge or connect or even enjoy a decent amount of sleep. And then it starts all over again the next day."

We all know your role in family and community life is vital, but when your own well-being comes last, of course you're going to feel tired and stressed, like Lindsey. Maybe you've even begun to feel invisible as a real, live human being with needs and desires of your own. Do you ever wonder if the people you serve really see you? Or do you feel like they've relegated you to simply playing a character in their own life story? Are you a real person to the boss who urgently needs an email drafted for a client, or to your 12 year old who just wants a ride to the mall? There's always one more zipper to help with... pair of shoes to tie... one more 16 year old who's out past curfew, and you suspect may have lied about where they were going... one more caller trying to reach someone else in the office... one more loving advance from your husband that feels a little less than loving... one more need to meet for someone else. I'm sure you have your own personal version of this!

And of course with busyness comes stress—health compromising, dream crushing, emotionally draining stress. And what do women do when they're stressed? Evolutionarily wired to be sure our kids are okay, we tend to try even harder to take care of everyone and everything else first. We want to make things all better, to rescue, to find safe landings for ourselves and the people we care for, at home and at work. We think if we move even faster and try even harder to control outcomes, then maybe all will be well. "I should be able to handle this." "I hate to ask for help because I know what needs to be done and can get it done in the time it'd take to explain to someone else." "It's easier to just do it myself." Does this sound familiar?

Self-care comes last—if it makes the list at all. But daydreams are filled with images of spa days, weekend retreats, or perhaps escaping to a cave in India. Lindsey's mantra early on in our work together was, "I. Need. A. Break." Underneath it was a deep cry, "What about me???"

At first, it seemed impossible for Lindsey to even consider the possibility of being able to figure out how to carve out time for herself. In those rare moments when there was a lull in the action, I knew she was more likely to catch up on sleep, numb out, or try to claw her way back to being on top of the pile of stuff on her to-do list. And I knew better than to suggest she get up half an hour earlier every morning to exercise, or meditate, or even drink her first cup of coffee in peace.

I also knew how to start introducing her to finding whole-ness right there in the midst of her hectic schedule. Lindsey wanted relief—some sense of peace—more than she wanted to stay stuck in the downward spiral of her stress, so she was willing to try doing things differently. Not with a behavior modification, stress management approach, but with tools, techniques, and connections that spoke to her soul and helped her reclaim a sense of wholeness for herself.

Don't get me wrong. Lindsey's still busy, but now she "magically" finds the time and space to take care of herself, nurture her true nature, and even pursue some of the things she loved doing before her life got so busy. She's rediscovering herself as an amazingly gifted woman, sepa-rate from her role identities as a wife, mom, and employee. You'll learn more about the "magic" and Lindsey's journey throughout the book.

We withdraw and isolate

Additionally, when you're overworked and overtired, it's hard to be as emotionally available as you want to be, as you're designed to be. We're natural born connectors, but when the stress is big enough, many women isolate emotionally. Our bodies may still be there, but emotion-ally we may be disconnected and far away. Then, watching ourselves withdraw from the people we love, we worry about the effect all that stress-laden unavailability has on our relationships. We feel guilty. Which adds another whole layer of stress.

Lindsey would say, "Other people have no idea how alone I feel." This from a woman whose early adulthood was marked by her well-developed friendships with other women. She also had strong bonds with her mom and her mom's friends. She knew the power of community.

She and three friends even organized an entire sledding journey across the Arctic, which necessitated a long process of working together to train dogs, gather equipment, map their course, and try to anticipate every contingency. Immersed in nature on that trip, they saw beauty and hardship, supported one another, overcame challenges and created deep friendships. Everything was done as a team, and Lindsey documented it all with her camera and with detailed journal entries. She felt alive and on track. Her life had meaning.

After the trek, Lindsey went to visit her mom, who was temporarily living in northern California. This is where she met her husband, who shared her love of the Arctic and of all things sledding. After they settled into his home and had children, her outside interests began fading into the background. She missed her friends, now scattered in other states. She didn't have the time or energy for frequent calls with them. She missed her mom and her mom's friends. She desperately wanted support, and had no idea how to find it, at least not without a radical move back to her hometown and mom. She said, "I know my mom and her friends love me. They would be there for me. That's how it's supposed to work, right?"

She found a bit of the adult connection she craved at her part-time job, which kept her from quitting that job long after the work itself no longer interested her.

She said, "I feel most alive when my best friend and I get out of town for the weekend, but she's busy, too, and it doesn't happen often enough."

As her busyness increased, so did her tendency to withdraw and isolate. Few, if any, others knew her innermost thoughts. She'd begun feeling awkward in everyday social interactions, unmoored from her deeper, relational life. She felt inauthentic in the brief interactions she was able to make happen. She deeply longed for more, while simultaneously feeling guilty for wanting more. She appreciated the life she was privileged to enjoy, and didn't want to appear ungrateful. She *was* grateful for what she had, but she also wanted more—so she bore the dissatisfaction silently, which drove her even deeper into withdrawal and isolation. This bind had kept her stuck for several years before she began to break through it.

When I invited Lindsey to join my mentoring program, a flicker of hope sparked in her hazel green eyes, along with a flash of what might have been rebellion against the status quo to which she been resigning herself. She accepted the invitation. With her husband, she worked out a way to free up the time at home, and made a solid commitment to participate. She felt out of place initially, unsure she really belonged there because most of the women were older and "wiser," in her eyes. But the group structure—including clear boundaries, unconditional acceptance and respect, and teachings about how to create wholeness in her life—helped her weave herself into the group. She began to share more of her inner world with the other women in the group, and found herself well-liked and accepted because of her openness. She grew to trust that she really does belong there. She has become an active voice in that group, grateful for the company of other women committed to growing healthy relationships with themselves, each other, their families, communities, and nature.

This is poignant: We say the answers lie within us, and they do. But some people think this means having to figure things out on their own and that asking for help is a sign of weakness. But this is never the way things work in nature. Nothing in nature grows independently from anything else. An aspen tree growing in the forest would not survive isolated from the resources around it. Light, water, soil, the nutrients in the soil, other plant life around it—all have an effect on how it grows. It's sad that humans think we have to go it alone, cut off from the very life force of resources all around us.

Clearly, there's no such thing as wholeness in isolation. If a genuine experience of wholeness reveals anything it is this: You are not alone. You do belong. And resources are everywhere! Hungry for real connection, we fare better in community as we find the missing pieces of our lives, tame our schedules, express ourselves authentically, and grow our gifts in the world. We're stronger when we walk together.

I suspect you know this. And if you're like other women I've met, you've tried to find your places of belonging, but chances are good you're still looking to fill in some gaps. You may have tried (or thought about trying) coaching, therapy, networking, yoga and meditation classes, women-only gatherings, art classes, dance classes, hiking groups or girls' nights out—and perhaps you've struggled to find the time to join in, or perhaps those groups didn't meet your hopes of finding others who are willing to be as authentic, open and loving as you wish to experience. Communities like those mentioned above can be very useful—a piece of the puzzle, but sometimes they don't meet our deepest needs for connection.

Keep reading and I think—I hope—you'll begin to sense that the original, indigenous understanding of wholeness has something more and different to offer.

But first, let's unfold a couple more challenges you may be facing.

Saying yes when we mean no

"For far too long we have been seduced into walking a path that did not lead us to ourselves. For far too long we have said yes when we wanted to say no. And for far too long we have said no when we desperately wanted to say yes...." Terry Tempest Williams says in her book, *When Women Were Birds*.

How often do you say yes when you really want to say no? How often do you say no to things you'd actually love to say yes to? And what happens when you don't honor what you really want? Do you end up feeling resentful because you think other people don't value you, or even think of you as a person, beyond appreciating what you may *do* for them? Worse, do you start questioning your own value?

Saying yes when you mean no, keeping yourself busy, taking care of others, all of this can make you wonder if your life has inherent meaning and value beyond to-do lists and making things happen for other people.

Yes, we're wired for compassion, but at what cost to our own well-being when caring for others becomes a primary source of identity—and thus of our sense of value? So many women have I heard say, "I don't know who I am anymore," and many of them are women who are willing to awaken and question the expectation our culture has placed upon them to serve others selflessly and smiling.

There is nothing inherently wrong with wanting to care for other people. That said, when it comes at the expense of your authentic responses in the moment and over time— *that* is a problem. The resulting incongruity can be devastating to your soul.

Do others know your innermost thoughts, or do you hide your real feelings, opinions or responses even from yourself? Do you smile when you do talk about your inner pain? Are you afraid that if other people knew what was really going on inside you, they'd think less of you? Have you experienced the double bind of being encouraged to be authentic and honest, but then been criticized or shamed for actually doing so?

Women who comply with the social and cultural expectations heaped upon them end up living a life that's out of alignment with their authentic ways of being—"seduced into walking a path that did not lead us to ourselves," as Terry Tempest Williams observed. And that's painful. Taken to an extreme, it can feel like there's literally no way out, short of running away and starting over somewhere fresh and new.

Ten years into her marriage, Lindsey was deeply entrenched in the effects of having said more yes's than she could gracefully manage, and not having said enough no's. When we first met, her face told of a sad, harried inner story of living a life that wasn't fully authentic. It showed in her body—stress lines, a distant look in her eyes, neck tense, shoulders drawn upward, tight pelvis.

It's not so much that Lindsey didn't want to say yes to the people she cared about—it's that she said it to an extreme. She believed it was her duty to enable possibility for others, because she was capable and could see solutions. But she didn't say yes to herself often enough. She didn't seem to have the time to remember and pursue her own gifts and passions, much less to meet her own needs for self-care.

This wasn't as true for Lindsey, but it is for some women, that even their big yes's can be deceptively out of alignment with their true selves. For a myriad of reasons, women sometimes make big choices, often early in life, that preclude them from actualizing who they really are. They say yes to a business major in college because it's what their parents wanted for them, yes to marrying a man who seemed to fit the bill for ideal but they didn't really love, yes to living in a place that doesn't bring them alive because it's close to their husband's job or their own next career move. How many of these big yes moves are made by young women seeking to hedge their bets on the uncertainties life offers? Or to please or appease someone else? No wonder we look back twenty, thirty, forty years later saying, "The life I'm living doesn't match the life I imagined for myself."

Fear of being seen

Another aspect of authenticity has to do with the tension between the *desire* to be seen for who we really are, and the *fear* of being seen for who we really are. When Lindsey began describing her pain to me, she'd smile. As if it wasn't okay to be seen as not okay. As if it wasn't okay to feel what she felt, and to express it congruently. No matter what was going on inside, the world would see a smile. Meanwhile, at home, she was often reactive and loud and tearful. But when she shared with me the pain of those times, and the events leading up to them, she smiled. She wanted to be perceived as capable and strong, not weak and stuck. Yet clearly she also wanted to be seen, acknowledged, and accepted in her pain, too, because she was willing to share with me information that was deeply personal and about which she felt embarrassed.

Being seen can be scary. And for some, it's downright terrifying, loaded with a fear of being exposed "for who I really am, a fraud." But even if there is some deep-seated sense inadequacy, self-doubt, or shame, that is certainly not a reflection of who you really are! It's actually a reflection of how much you had to hide and shapeshift in order to be valued and perceived as lovable while you were growing up. It reflects a fear of being seen as "not enough," or perhaps as "too much," if you were to reveal more of your inner world—darkness and light, weakness and power.

How would your life be different if you felt completely loved and accepted just as you are, flaws and strengths and all? Can you imagine how much more courageously you might show up if you were able to tap into that kind of love and acceptance in an ongoing way?

We're going to be exploring a kind of wholeness that includes plugging into the world around you—feet on the ground, heart-centered, and whole—and brings with it the kind of love and acceptance you long for, creating a rooted experience of presence, of knowing where you stand and confidently using your voice to express your truth.

As we learn how to plug into the land, we begin to step into authentic wholeness the way our indigenously living sisters experience it. Plugging into the land they way they do will help clarify your real yes's and no's—opening the way for authentic expression of your passion, purpose, and power. If you've ever spent a few days in the wilderness, close to the land, you know what I'm talking about. You know how transformative it is to connect with nature in an ongoing way. The clarity, creativity, and ease that begin to emerge.

Forgotten dreams

Lindsey knew what she wanted in life. Things weren't perfect in her 20's and 30's, but she had earned a degree in photojournalism and developed a deep love of documenting her time in the wilderness, and was creating a viable means of realizing her dreams as she led wilderness expeditions for teenage girls. These adventures also fulfilled her desire to make a difference in the lives of girls who sometimes struggled, as she did, as a teenager. Immersed in nature on those trips, they saw beauty and hardship, overcame challenges and created deep friendships.

Then, hmmm... what happened? How, she wondered, did she end up married with two kids and a job serving somebody else's dreams? She loved her family, but in devoting all of herself to taking care of them, she'd abandoned and forgotten other important aspects of herself.

And when I first asked her what she's passionate about, what her big dreams are, Lindsey said, "I have no idea what my passion is." That's how far she had veered from her authentic, central vision and passion for making a difference in the world, as well as for her family.

Have your biggest dreams faded to background, too—that sense of mission, something important you know you're here to contribute to? Do you remember being (as Rumi puts it) "drawn by the silent pull of what you really love?" Even if you couldn't quite put it into words, the future looked bright. Do you ever look back nostalgically, imagining what could have been if you'd made different choices, or maybe concluding that dreams are the stuff of youth—not a realistic guide for real life? Do you long to breathe new life into those forever dreams and find out where they might still take you?

Even with all the permission overtly granted us to pursue our dreams today, many of the women who come through my mentoring program don't know what they want to do when they "grow up,"—even at 40, 50 and 60+ years old. Some do, but others either have no idea, are afraid to speak it, or have relegated their dreams to the background while living lives of quiet longing for passion and freedom. Do any of these descriptions fit for you, too? If so, beyond a shadow of a doubt I know that the seeds of your dreams are there inside you, waiting to be rediscovered and grown to fruition, even if you have ventured off course.

CHAPTER TWO

Why Wholeness?

...and then the day came when the risk to remain tight in a bud was more painful than the risk it took to blossom. **ANAIS NIN**

My journey

Emerging from a stressful childhood, as the oldest of five girls, I faced a long healing process to deal with the ungrieved death of my youngest sister, the effects of growing up with overwhelmed parents, a pattern of dissociating from my feelings, and a tendency to disappear behind a smile in relationship with others. One of my coping mechanisms was to put others' needs first. To disappoint anyone was painful, a culpability that heaped shame upon my already fragile sense of identity, so I did everything I could to avoid it.

I was bright enough to figure out what others needed, and to adjust my behaviors to fit others' needs and expectations, even before I could walk and talk. I became self-sufficient really young, more than willing to do things for myself, without help.

I was also afraid. Not only of being seen (because I was quite shy), but of some unseen force lurking in the dark that haunted my sleep well into adulthood.

I felt very much alone in the world, despite the outward appearance of a happy family and active social life. No one would have guessed the private hell I was living... not even me.

My escape was upward into the world of pure Spirit, made easy by the blessing of growing up with a God who was not anthropomorphized. In the Christian Science religion of my youth, God was Father/Mother, yes, but not in a human sense—more in an archetypal way. And more than that, God was synonymous with Love. And Spirit. And Life, Truth, and Soul. It was in this world that I found my greatest comfort and joy, although I also disconnected from my physical body, dissociated from my human needs and emotions.

Eventually, something inside started to wake back up. I made a few bold (for me) choices, and was given a bit of grace. Walking the halls of my high school between classes, I decided one day to raise my gaze from the floor and greet people eye to eye, saying, "Hi!" I became active with a local church youth group. I worked summers at a Colorado camp where I discovered a deep sense of belonging and family, and I was seen as a leader. I was accepted to attend a college exclusively for Christian Scientists, where I was lovingly received into some very nurturing circles. I had one-of-a-kind opportunities to travel overseas and spend time in the wilderness of Colorado and Wyoming, expanding both my worldview and my sense of self-confidence.

In my mid-20's I moved to Colorado, and left behind the study of Christian Science, sensing that something important was missing in my exploration. I was ready for a fresh start and to find my own way to Truth, whatever that meant. This included study of other spiritual paths, getting some counseling, and lots of introspection.

Flash forward a few years, as I fell in love with a wonderful man and natural born healer/therapist, and moved in with him. At the time, I was working in the front office of a busy mental health clinic, answering phones, managing therapist schedules, and fielding emergencies. Feeding off the stress there, my whole life began to feel like an emergency, loaded with a sense of urgency and impending doom if I didn't get everything done.

I know what it's like to make a to-do list and not be able to rest until everything is checked off. I know what it's like to not get everything done and experience the stress that comes with unfinished business. I remember what it's like to have friends over for dinner, looking more and more like a crazy woman as their arrival time drew near, because the house "had" to be in perfect order.

I know what it's like to smile my way through a grocery store conversation I don't really want to have because I'm in such a hurry. Or to pretend I don't even see that old friend in the produce section, no matter how much I like her.

I know what it's like to want the best for the children in your life, to adjust and adapt your own wants and needs to try and meet theirs, to navigate co-parenting when each parental figure has their own vision of what constitutes adequate support or proper discipline. Even though I didn't have children of my own, my stepson was barely a teenager when I moved in with his dad. He was fresh off his parents' divorce and processing all the grief, anger, and hardship divorce brings for a child.

I know what it's like to long for a break. For the chance to sit in the sun with a good book. Or to actually use that gift certificate for a massage. Or take a vacation... without the kids. Maybe even without the spouse.

I remember what it was like to put a smile on my face when everything in me wanted to cry. Or lash out in anger.

I know what it's like to feel stuck in a world of demands and expectations that leave you feeling drained, convinced you just don't have what it takes to simplify your life.

At the height of my overworked, overextended, over-whelmed life circumstances, I decided to listen more deeply to the call of what my soul really wanted.

You see, I've always had this crazy strong sense of calling—of mission and vision, and I've never been able to ignore it! It's one thing that has kept me ever hopeful and optimistic even in the most challenging of times. It's not that I knew what I wanted to be when I grew up. I didn't. It's that the calling itself was so strong it eventually became a source of guidance to find my real work. In my late thirties, I decided to follow the call as best I could, one step at a time.

For awhile, things got even crazier. I went back to school for a Master's degree in Counseling, while working full time and starting another intense training program at the same time. In the summer of 1990, I finished grad school, had my wisdom teeth pulled while I still had insurance (one of them impacted), quit my job at the mental health center, started a private practice, crashed and burned on my bicycle (requiring exquisite plastic surgery to save my face), and got married.

The next few years were all about re-establishing myself in my new roles growing a marriage and a business, and learning all the usual tips and tools for managing stress and overcoming codependence (the pattern of looking outside oneself for a sense of okayness and validation). I continued to explore my lifelong interest in spirituality. I also began a process of profound healing to free myself from the effects of years of deep wounding. I believe that any courageous journey of becoming requires us to do at least some healing work. (I am passionate about the healing aspect of the journey, which is covered in depth in my first book, *Reclaiming Wholeness*, along with other topics touched on in this chapter.)

Introducing wholeness

Pursuing my interest in spirituality eventually drew me to Peru and the Andean traditions, where wholeness and community exist hand in hand, inextricably part of a way of life. There I found beautiful role models of original, indigenous understandings of wholeness that are surprisingly relevant for Western culture today: getting our own lives in order, showing up authentically, realizing our dreams, and learning how to thrive even under stressful conditions.

I learned that wholeness starts with a great big taproot into the land. A beautifully poetic way of saying this and a core teaching of the Andean lineages, is that "the land speaks us into being." Indigenous peoples have always known the land is alive and conscious, that human presence emerges from Spirit through the land, and that the connection can't actually be cut (except perhaps by our lack of awareness of the connection).

I began learning a lot more about this kind of wholeness when I joined Marti Spiegelman's training program, Shamans' Light™. It started with a few simple awareness exercises out in nature—noticing beauty; registering colors, textures, sounds; breathing the energies of earth, sunlight, and air into my body; sinking my roots into the soil; even spending an hour in nature every day for a year. (Toward the back of the book, in Appendix A, you'll find some earth-based practices to help with your own exploration of wholeness.)

The more I did these exercises and practiced organizing my life around wholeness, the more solid I began to feel—more confident, more able to handle stressors, more able to be present right where I was (no matter how uncomfortable). I became better able to notice when I was over-giving so I could course-correct. I grew increasingly clear about what I wanted for myself, both personally and professionally.

As my connection to Earth deepened, so did my connection to Spirit. I learned how to source the world of Spirit to grow and develop my human life. My big but at the time still unfocused longing to change the world began to take shape as the work I now do with the training and mentoring program I founded after closing my counseling practice several years ago. The Wholeness Project™ is devoted to helping other people with big vision and big longings to shape their lives in alignment with their real passions and purpose.

Perhaps most importantly, I discovered in my relationship with Pachamama (Mother Earth, our "one, true mother,"), a profound sense of being loved and lovable, no matter what else was going on around me.

Radical grounding

One aspect of wholeness I've been investigating for several years has to do with reconnecting roots to the land where you were born. I discovered that our birthplaces hold important clues to individual identity, passion, and purpose. I learned a lot about myself through a process of reconnecting to my own roots, so I started sharing it with others. When those people made equally profound discoveries to my own, I got excited. I named the process "Radical Grounding," and I've had the joy of witnessing many people breathe new life into their dreams and refine their life's work simply by reconnecting to their original roots through the process of Radical Grounding.

That the land where you were born has anything to do with why you're here may sound like a radical claim to make— and it is. Most of us have been transplanted several times over away from our places of birth and don't even think to consider the magic lying latent in the land there. But the magic and wisdom encoded in those original landscapes have always been there, completely available to tap back into.

Are you up for playing with me a bit here? This is a fun way to learn more about your purpose. We're going to take a look at the land where you were born—specifically, to the geographies and forces that shaped the natural landscape where you were born. The place where you emerged onto the planet is informed by the surrounding landscape and so, as a part of that natural world, you are also informed by the energies of that land.

When you left your birthplace, it was as if you were transplanted, cut off from roots that are still there for you to reconnect with now. In those original roots, a chunk of your magic lies waiting for you to show up and reclaim it.

For an initial taste of Radical Grounding, try this simple exercise. It's where most people start exploring. Stand outside, on the earth. If you have a yard or can get to a park or other natural surroundings, it would be ideal. If you're in the middle of a big city, use your imagination to make the buildings and concrete disappear so you can sense what the land was like before all the building arrived. You can actually do this anywhere!

Imagine you have roots growing out of the soles of your feet, grounding you right where you are. Tune in to the energies of the land around you—all your senses wide open to experience that land as fully as possible. Then, turn up your imagination and sense your root system stretching back to your birthplace. Back to the land through which you were born. Take some time to experience what it's like to reconnect your roots—stretching for a sense of seamless connection that unfolds as you send your roots all the way back to their source in your birthplace.

From here, you could then take a closer look at the actual landforms of your birthplace (mountain, river, forests, lake, desert, ocean, etc.), in order to learn more about how those landforms can (and do) inform your purpose and passion. For instance, born near a river you may know a lot about going with the flow and how to carve a riverbed, even if you haven't yet developed these capacities. Born in the mountains, you may know a lot about high-level vision and what it takes to go from the valley floor to the mountaintop. We first connect with the landforms and then practice embodying and being those landforms. Being the river, mountain, prairie, lake, glacial till with increasing specificity.

These are general observations, with details emerging as you explore the geography more thoroughly in relation to your own life, taking the time to uncover the specific powers of those landforms that inform who you are and what you came to do, finding your authentic gifts reflected back to you. Through Radical Grounding, you get to learn a lot about how you belong—that in addition to your human communities, you belong to a region of collective consciousness that's expressed in the land where you were born. It's a connection that brings you present—seeing and being seen, loving and being loved. It's a connection that creates original, indigenous wholeness.

To be whole is to...

Now twenty years into my exploration of this kind of wholeness, I've become convinced that our indigenous sisters' and brothers' understanding is vitally important for the well-being of western culture. Their understanding is so beautifully comprehensive it seems to leave no missing piece to the puzzle of how we might free ourselves from the challenges of being too busy, too isolated, and too discon-nected from our dreams to create the lives we've imagined.

Howard Thurman once said, "Don't ask yourself what the world needs; ask yourself what makes you come alive. And then go and do that. Because what the world needs is people who have come alive."

To which I would add: "Because when you're doing 'what makes you come alive' you're *being* what you were created for, and *that*'s what the world needs." That's a vital aspect of wholeness.

This new/old understanding of original wholeness will meet you exactly where you are and help you grow from there. It's both practical and profound.

To be whole is to...

- take exquisite care of yourself

- be grounded, present, awake, and aware

- say yes when you mean yes, no when you mean no

- know what you love and go for it

- recognize fertile ground for right action in the moment

- wake up as an integral part of the kinship of all life

- claim your vital presence, your voice, your work in the world

- let your light shine

- flourish

CHAPTER THREE

Why Women?

She is as full of beautiful possibilities as a perfect harp, and she realizes that all the harmonies of the universe are in herself, while her own soul plays upon magic strings the unwritten anthems of Love.

MARY BAKER EDDY

Our role moving forward

At the Vancouver Peace Summit in 2009, the Dalai Lama said, "The world will be saved by the Western woman."

His message echoes what we have also heard from other teachers (men and women) in indigenous cultures: that the next evolutionary wave of wisdom will come from the West, and be led by women. In the Andes, this is understood to mean that the re-instatement of the feminine principle is key to western culture taking the lead now.

So, why women? Why the feminine?

I hope you'll recognize yourself, or at least your potential, in this chapter. We're asking, "why women," but the real question is, why *you*?

As women, we are very specially designed for creating well-being for ourselves and our loved ones, and for planting seeds of well-being in our communities.

We have an intuitive way of tuning in, listening, and responding to others.

Women are naturally receptive. Our bodies are designed to receive.

We are channels for streams of wisdom flowing into the world.

As women, we inherently know how to give birth (to babies, ideas, projects....)

We have a keen ability to recognize fertility when we see it.

We're able to hold multiple viewpoints at once.

We have an intuitive sense of cycles and timings because our own cycles are intimately connected to the cycles of the moon and the ebb and flow of the ocean.

Our true nature is love.

Women's bodies are designed to receive input from outside and then to create something with it—new life catalyzed when egg and sperm say yes to each other. We're designed to recognize a good match, to receive the spark that catalyzes something totally new to come into being from the union.

We're designed to embrace and embody the mystery, to listen deeply and allow all that is unknown to remain unknown until it rises naturally and of its own accord.

We don't necessarily live this way, but we're designed for it.

That's what I know.

A download

When I arrived to this point in writing this chapter, I got stuck, not knowing what to say or how to add to the conversation. Churning inside, I was fearful that perhaps I had nothing new to contribute, and that maybe I didn't really have a whole book to write after all.

The muse seemed far away. I couldn't find my way into the mystery from which the best discoveries emerge. I tried writing with my non-dominant hand, as is sometimes suggested to free blocking. I tried free-writing, journaling with no particular structure or thought process to support it, just writing whatever wanted to come. I got drowsy. In fact I'd been staving off drowsiness for more than an hour.

At first, I judged the drowsiness. Sure, I could go to sleep. I could choose to numb out and not allow the muse to speak through. Wall's up, can't get through, I'm going to sleep.

But finally, Spirit got through to me as I remembered other times I'd felt drowsy in the middle of the day and recognized it as a message to go lie down, get out of the way, and let magic happen. What if this was Spirit's way of getting through to me again? "Incoming! We have information and knowledge for you. Go lie down. This is how we're going to deliver the rest of this chapter."

So I paused... took a deep breath... and walked straight into the mystery.

With a crystal in my left hand, I laid down on the futon in my office, my sacred tools beside me, left hand reaching into the mystery, and holding the question, "Why women?"

Tears rose in my eyes, as the message began pouring in. "Because we carry the grief. The feminine is associated with the waters, deep waters, salt waters of Mother Ocean. Your tears are salty like the waters of the sea. Women hold the remembrance of how things used to be, when the feminine and masculine principles weren't divided between men and women, when we accepted that everyone carries aspects of both."

(The Dagara people of Africa see tears as sacred: "the heart coming to the eyes so it can see better.")

The download continued to flow in: "Women know the wound of separation. We know the wound because we have lived it, lived in a world dominated by a short-sighted view of the masculine—going for the riches, each man for himself, pillaging the Earth for Her precious resources in order to live well himself. It's been too much *I, I, I,* with woman expected to be the support system at home and at work, no matter what else she's engaged in. Cut off from and devaluing the feminine, men (and women) have forgotten the value of the feminine principle itself.

"Women know this because we've lived it and lost our voice to change things. That is changing now. It has already changed dramatically, but there is so much more to be done. Our voices are re-emerging, as they must, because the old way is no longer working.

"We could view this as a long and necessary swing from one pole of being (masculine dominance) to the other (feminine dominance), but that's not the answer.

"Some men may fear the coming changes because they're afraid they won't be valued, or that they'll lose something important. And they certainly do not want to be dominated any more than women do. Simply reversing roles is clearly not the answer.

"The real problem is that the masculine has been operating separate from the feminine. The masculine has done this really amazing thing of unplugging itself from the feminine. That's not the way nature works, but as humans we have an added special ability to think strategically about things—and mess with nature. As a principle in nature, the feminine and masculine operate as one thing. It's impossible to have one without the other. Only the strategic mind could possibly concoct a way to separate the two and then think it was a good idea! Disconnecting the two has profoundly affected our relationships, our politics, and our treatment of Mother Earth. In today's world, the masculine generally doesn't even know where to look for the feminine, and women are beginning to raise their voices to say this is no longer okay.

"The answer lies in reuniting the masculine and feminine as one principle. The answer lies in each person recovering within himself or herself a fully working system of the feminine and the masculine together. The feminine informing the masculine. Not women informing men, but men developing the ability to tap into the mystery as women so naturally do, and finding guidance for their actions in the world. And women developing the ability to tap into their own dynamic nature so their capacity to manifest is naturally informed by the feminine and sparked by the masculine. Split from this natural informing and sparking, humans have created a way of being that simply isn't sustainable."

Rejoining the feminine and masculine

The download complete, I remembered Marti Spiegelman talking about the feminine and the masculine in her shamanic consciousness trainings:

> *A useful thing to remember is Angeles Arrien's beautiful metaphor of the pool of oil and the flaming torch. Imagine a pool of oil to the left and a flaming torch to the right. The oil travels from the pool along a wick to the torch, and the flame is only there because of the pool of oil. If you cut the wick—which is cutting the link between the Feminine and the Masculine, the flame is going to burn up and burn out. No longer informed by the Feminine, Masculine energies of the flame can even become unconsciously destructive. When the dynamic energy in you is no longer informed or*

fed by the Feminine energy, you tend to burn up, or burn out. So if this happens to you, if you end up as the torch with no wick, at the very least you may say to yourself 'My God, I've got no resources left.'

On the other side, is the pool of oil, which is the Feminine— the fuel for expression, the visionary, the fluid. If the wick is cut, you can drown in the unexpressed, in overwhelm. If you have vision that can't be expressed [as the flame expresses the oil], you won't experience well-being. If all you have is energy that cannot be crafted into vision, that energy will likely express in its own destructive ways–as the shadow side of the Feminine. This shadow energy tends to become subversive. All the evil mothers who subvert by not loving. Without words, doing damage by withdrawing love, withdrawing connection, creating such emotional damage covertly. That's the shadow of the Feminine.

Women are being called to provide this next evolutionary push because we're the ones with the wisdom in our bellies to heal the split between the masculine and the feminine. We're the ones empowered and available enough to start restoring the original meaning of wholeness that's been held hostage in a culture that values the masculine over the feminine.

This doesn't make men irrelevant on our evolutionary journey—their role is emerging, too. I certainly don't think the call is limited only to women. There are some amazing, beautiful men waking up to the deeper wisdom they carry and are meant to bring to the transformative process before us. They, too, are healing. They, too, are reweaving a more respectful, generative experience of both the feminine and masculine principle into their ways of being.

Why women? Because we're made for this. We're ready for this. Our time is now.

CHAPTER FOUR

Why Walking?

Walking in the woods, I felt in touch with the universe and with the spirit of the universe.
ALICE WALKER

Wholeness is a verb

When we talk about "walking in wholeness," we're talking about an active engagement with Earth and Spirit that opens channels of creativity and creation. Wholeness is much more verb than noun. It's a way of being that draws from the Feminine/Masculine principle as one thing—oil and flame, vision and action, as one system. If we're not active—if we aren't walking in wholeness—then we're not really *whole*.

Let's look first at the literal act of walking and then ease into a more metaphorical use of the word.

When we walk, we feel better. The whole nervous system gets involved. There's a very cool little book by Thom Hartmann titled *Walking Your Blues Away* that documents the effectiveness of bilateral stimulation (one foot in front of the other, opposite arm swinging forward, both hemispheres of the brain engaged and stimulated) for optimal processing and well-being.

Then there's the Wallace Stevens saying: "Perhaps the truth depends on a walk around the lake." This is often true for me. When I get stuck, or thinking feels murky and slow, or I feel unmotivated to take on some task, a walk breaks things loose so I can think clearly again. The real art is to drop thinking altogether, notice the beauty all around, and swing those arms. This is why I typically prefer to walk alone. It typically does my heart, soul, and mind more good to walk quietly than to be talking, unless my walking partner is equally open to the natural world around us.

I am with Henry David Thoreau when he declares in his book on *Walking*,

> *"I am alarmed when it happens that I have walked a mile into the woods bodily, without getting there in spirit. In my afternoon walk I would fain forget all my morning occupations and my obligations to society. But it sometimes happens that I cannot easily shake off the village. The thought of some work will run in my head, and I am not where my body is—I am out of my senses. In my walks I would fain return to my senses. What business have I in the woods, if I am thinking of something out of the woods?"*

We so often walk with little or no awareness of the earth beneath our feet, stuck in our heads and thinking about other things. If we decide to actually "take a walk," it's often as much a purposeful activity to work off accumulated stresses or negative energies, as it is to be outside breathing fresh air and noticing Mother Nature's beauty all around.

But walking *is* about being out of doors, preferably in nature, surrounded by beauty. Here's what happens when we walk consciously:

We walk to remember our own beauty, reflected to us all around.

We walk to declare our presence.

We walk to remember the truth in our bones.

We walk to soar. We walk so the ground becomes real beneath our feet, solid enough there's something to push off from, so we can fly.

We walk because that's where our *souls* meet earth: through our *soles*.

We walk to sense the conversation between our feet and the earth. It's where the architecture of your spirit plugs into the grid of creation. We walk to bring awareness to the conversation unfolding there so we can remember our place in the family of all that is—so we can remember our true identity as sons and daughters of the land, our voices informed by the magic we find at our feet.

We walk to listen deeply to the land that speaks us into being.

We walk to reclaim our birthright of wholeness. There is no wholeness without walking, without dynamic action. We walk into wholeness—we don't *think* our way into wholeness.

Wholeness is active and alive and ever available to tap into. It isn't static.

And when we walk and talk with one another as emergent expressions of the land, then the conversation has meaning and depth beyond what we might have thought possible. As the poet Rumi said,

> *Out beyond ideas of wrongdoing and rightdoing,*
> *there is a field. I'll meet you there.*

> *When the soul lies down in that grass,*
> *the world is too full to talk about.*
> *Ideas, language, even the phrase "each other"*
> *doesn't make any sense.*

Thinking will mess you up

But we live in a culture that values thinking over being. We strategize our way forward. We try to "figure out" our next steps, a skill most of us developed in order to navigate the world of childhood. Many kids (perhaps you were one?) are highly gifted at figuring out what other people needed from them, and then how to meet the need. When simply being our sweet, innocent selves wasn't enough to ensure belonging, we were bright enough to strategize how to show up so our caregivers would love us and take care of us, so we'd be okay. For some, it was a matter of survival. And today, we still overly rely on that same strategic thinking skill to try to free ourselves from the well-engrained pattern of figuring out what others might need and taking care of them at the expense of our own well-being.

In a quote often attributed to Einstein, Bob Samples said (referencing Einstein's work), "The intuitive mind is a sacred gift and the rational mind a faithful servant. We have created a society that honors the servant and has forgotten the gift." It may be with good reason that we've come to value the rational, thinking mind over the vast resources of other parts of the brain, but it's not an optimal use of the gifts we've been given.

There is no prefigured template for well-being. We cannot think our way into well-being with our advanced cognition, by figuring things out. The sacred gift of the "intuitive" mind becomes available only through being, not through thinking.

As we master states of beingness, the thinking mind can then help us express what we've experienced, but it's never the source of experience. When you say, "I have a dream," the source of the dream lies in the realm of the intuitive mind. The dream resides in a magical realm, accessible only when you're relaxed and present in full consciousness—out beyond the world of thoughts and thinking. It's accessible only in full beingness.

Linking walking and being

One way to develop the capacity to *just be*—in relationship with the land—is to walk. When we're *being* rather than thinking, we're awake and present and can be in relationship with the land around us.

Why is it important to be in relationship with the land around us? Because, as Joseph Campbell reminds us, (and indigenous peoples have always known), the land is alive. The land is conscious. And, as we're beginning to remember, we are spoken into being through the land—both in an original sense (through the geographies of our birthplace) and from moment to moment. We're never separate.

One especially palpable experience of oneness with the land occurred when I participated in a wilderness retreat led by a Peruvian shaman, in the mid 1990's. A group of about 15 had gathered on Colorado's eastern front of the Rocky Mountains, amid towering spruce and pine trees, rocky outcroppings, and fertile forest soil covered with dried pine needles. Each day included a period of meditation, sitting in and with the natural world around us.

Feeling very alive on the final day of the retreat, I felt compelled to do a walking meditation in a shallow, seasonally dry creek bed. I wanted to feel my bare feet on the forest floor, to converse with Mother Earth, sole to soul. I stood quietly at first, just feeling the contact between my feet and the land beneath them, soaking in the energies pouring forth from the spot where I stood. Then very slowly I lifted one foot, sensing each micro movement—the way the energy between us remained unbroken, strands of energy connecting my foot to earth even when we weren't 'touching,' the way those strands shifted ever so slightly, the higher my foot rose, without ever disconnecting, then slowly placing the foot back on earth a bit ahead of the other one.

With each step, the relationship deepened. Like we were getting to know each other. Like I was letting myself be seen and known in a whole new way. Like I was experiencing my being emerge through those strands of energy, spoken into being through the land, integrally woven into the forested land all around.

So, I use 'walking' here as a metaphor for actively connecting to earth, to nature's wisdom, to the wellspring of your own true nature. There is actual walking involved in our work, but it's in service of remembering our inseparability from nature, and making discoveries about how to take dynamic action that sources from a deep wellspring. We "walk" the knowledge of wholeness into our bones, by practicing until the experience is fully embodied. Then we practice living it.

When you go for a walk, use it as an opportunity to feel the connection between your feet and the earth. Use it as an opportunity to focus on beauty. Imagine yourself as a big receiving dish tuned in to the natural world, and see if you can sense the land speaking you into being. Practice the slow, conscious, connected walking I described above.

Actively nurturing your connection to Mother Earth brings the most profound sense of belonging imaginable. I think we actually remember our old indigenous souls through spending time outdoors, in nature, bringing awareness to the energies around us. I believe this is where we start waking up in wholeness—by bringing ourselves fully present, aware, and available to all the wisdom streaming through Mother Nature's veins and into our own.

In earth-anchored wholeness, the stress that comes with *thinking* and *doing*, split from direct experience of our surroundings, is replaced with a profound sense of *being*, and even *being okay*.

In earth-anchored wholeness, your relationship to the to-do list flips on its head and inside out, while stuff gets done in good timing, with ease, because your doing is connected to and rises from the field of being. As Lindsey practiced earth-anchored wholeness, she reported feeling less of the anxiety and pressure that had characterized her life for so long. Hurriedly chopping onions as she rushed to get dinner on the table one night, she realized she had a choice. "The onions are going to get chopped—am I going to show up for it?"

In earth-anchored wholeness, the existential questions about who you are and where you belong dissolve, replaced by an experience of radical aliveness, along with deeply knowing your true nature and your true places of belonging.

Walking together

Can you imagine being part of a community of women where profound presence, belonging, and dynamic action are practiced and nurtured by everyone—each woman walking into a clearer sense of her passion and purpose and realizing her dreams with the support of like-hearted women? Imagine being seen by others in the light of your true nature. Imagine the acceptance, the love, and the power of a group of visionary women choosing to connect in this way. Imagine finding a place where your dreams can be planted, tended, and grown to fruition, with all the right nutrients.

The potential of a community of like-minded women to make things happen is exponentially greater than what any one of us could accomplish alone. In a community like this, the magical powers of nature and of Spirit come out to play, too, in support of each individual participant and in support of the collective.

In a community like this, you'll find the kind of resonance or complementarity with one another that prepares you for taking whatever small steps or quantum leaps you need to take to create real change in your life.

Let's walk together out of our isolated individual lives and into a world of full possibility.

Let's claim our birthrights to be seen (even when it's scary), to be loved (even when we're challenged), and to revitalize our dreams (even when they seem out of reach).

Let's clear whatever is blocking authentic expression of our true needs and desires and find ways to support our loved ones that doesn't squelch our own dreams.

Let's co-create a world in which all people—women and men—know they belong and know their individual contributions have meaning and value.

Let's walk together in wholeness.

CHAPTER FIVE

Why Community?

Thriving is a collective state. **MARTI SPIEGELMAN**

This is the structure of the narrative we're unfolding: *Why women*? *Why walking*? *Why wholeness*? But it's a fluid structure. The three go hand in hand if we're to change the world the way we want to. They can't be separated. A conversation occurs between the three, and something bigger emerges, something beyond but including each aspect. "Women walking in wholeness" is more about the multidimensional synthesis of the three than it is about each of the questions. It's the place where words become real, where dreams find their roots, where identity is about more than your personal history, facts and intangible factors that have impacted your life. It's the place where identity is shaped and called forth to create its future. It's also the place where we remember and reclaim the way in which we belong to the world.

The big context

Let's walk together into an expanded understanding of community. To set the stage, we'll start with a journey of discovery as a reminder of just how big the context of our lives really is.

For the next few minutes, you're invited to imagine yourself traveling from the place where you're sitting right now into the outer reaches of the cosmos. Allow as much time as you'd like for this exercise. At least five or ten minutes would be ideal!

Take a moment first to notice how you're experiencing yourself in relation to your own body, and to center yourself in a couple of deep relaxed breaths. As you feel your body, just as it is, you can notice that it's a unit, one thing—head, shoulders, arms, torso, pelvis, legs, feet, all one thing making your physical presence. You. Imagine you're a great big receiving dish— seeing, hearing, sensing, smelling, tasting. All you.

Now sense the environment around you. Your home, office, coffee shop, yard.... Wherever you are, bring awareness to your immediate surroundings.

Now, expand your awareness to include the neighborhood around you. And then your town.

Now, expand your awareness to the geographic region around you.... And your country.... Expand further to include the continent... then the entire planet.

Now keep going. Let your awareness take in the sun and moon and stars, our solar system.... The Milky Way.... Notice that the Milky Way sits in an even larger context of other galaxies.

Hang out in the expansiveness of space for a moment or two or ten, taking in the vastness of the universes in which we live and move and have our being.

Then, very slowly, begin to bring your awareness back in, bringing the sense of vastness with you.... Through the Milky Way.... Back through our solar system.... To planet Earth.

Bring your awareness back through your continent.... Your country.... The geographic region around you.... Your town.... and neighborhood.

Find yourself once again in your immediate surroundings, in your body, fully rooted and grounded. You. Seeing, hearing, sensing, smelling, tasting. And still breathing in the vastness of the journey you've been on. Expansive and grounded at the same time.

Sit quietly for a few moments, simply noticing without thinking.

Cosmologist Thomas Berry says, "A spirituality is a mode of being in which not only the divine and the human commune with each other, but we discover ourselves in the universe and the universe discovers itself in us." I suspect you know that every cell of your body, every part of you, has its origins in stardust. So when you expand awareness out into the universe, you're revisiting your original home, tapping into the consciousness out of which you emerge on earth moment to moment to moment. And when you gaze up at the stars at night from your front porch, you're seeing your ancestors and something of your own essence. You're looking out into the cosmos of which you are a part.

I'm sharing this visualization because it so compellingly creates an experience of greater belonging and an innate connection to everything in the known universe and beyond. This is the really big context in which our individual, familial, and community lives are unfolding today. From the micro to the macro, everything is part of a greater whole. Everything is collective.

Nurturing collectivity

Let's now bring the conversation back to the more micro— our everyday human lives and communities.

A line from an Al Green tune pops into my awareness: "I'm so tired of being along, so tired here on my own..." and merges with a line from an old Beatles tune, "Won't you please, please help me?" Do you ever feel this way? Tired of being too busy to pause and breathe and remember your own soul? Wishing someone would come along, offer to help, and lighten your load?

When we're caught up in the isolation of a too busy life, the world looks flat. Passion lies dormant on the outer edges of awareness. And the sense of tribe we crave can seem far, far away.

But just as all of nature operates collectively (and we are an integral part of nature) humans are naturally collective, with women like you and me hopefully leading the way back to the healing power of community.

There's no substitute for connection with women who know and love you. It's one of those things that we simply must claim the time and space for on a regular basis. The chance to connect deeply with other women and explore what it's like to walk in wholeness again, needs to be woven into the very fabric of our lives in order for us to do the work we're called to do in the world.

As we find our tribes another miraculous thing starts to happen: we get to be seen for who we *wholly* are—souls in possession of beautiful gifts, beautiful flaws, and all. Elizabeth Gilbert, author of *Big Magic*, says, "To be fully seen by someone, then to be loved anyway–this is a human offering that can border on the miraculous." To be fully seen and loved seems miraculous because something in us may have believed such an experience to be impossible. But it's actually our birthright. And I think it also feels miraculous because it is so deeply healing for our psyches and souls, hungry to be seen and loved.

Along these lines, the indigenous teacher, Malidoma Somé says,

> "*Whether they are raised in indigenous or modern culture, there are two things that people crave: the full realization of their innate gifts, and to have these gifts approved,*

*acknowledged, and confirmed. There are countless people
in the West whose efforts are sadly wasted because they have
no means of expressing their unique genius. In the psyches
of such people there is an inner power and authority that
fails to shine because the world around them is blind to it."*

When your gifts are "approved, acknowledged, and confirmed," by others, they grow. You grow. No more wasted efforts because you "have no means of expressing your unique genius!"

The caveat to this is that being fully seen can also be frightening. You will come face to face with your own power and beauty! It may take some time, tenderness, and compassionate healing to grow into full ownership of your full potential.

A group of women recently gathered in my office to celebrate the close of a mentoring year as participants in my *Women Walking in Wholeness* training program, which focused on helping them remember their authentic gifts of passion, purpose, and power. They shared their most sacred discoveries and thanks with one another. Here's a sampling:

*"I am embracing my authenticity, and you all are witness
to it. I feel accepted and honored in a heartfelt place that
honors who I am."*

*"You accept me for who I am and that lessens my fear. I
love the positive support we get here; it's never demeaning
or negative. I really believe we have been chosen by the*

spirits, the universe, and when we get together it's to find out what for."

"When we come together, I'm aware of a greater wisdom that we tap into, a wisdom that isn't as available just working on my own. I can feel support coming in that wasn't there before. I've got tools—actual ways to tap into that wisdom, and I'm practicing and using the tools you give us."

When women walk together in wholeness, love comes alive. You stop comparing yourself to others, and instead show up ready and willing to participate in your life and your tribe. You remember who you really are.

When women walk together in wholeness, you stand in your authentic individuality as a valued member of the community. No shapeshifting is required for acceptance and recognition.

When women walk together in wholeness, connection is not based in merging with one another, but in being fully yourself in relation to other women being fully themselves.

When women walk together in wholeness, your actions are in service of creating well-being for all.

When women walk together in wholeness, the feminine and masculine come alive within you, through which you are then able to create states of thriving.

Ayllu

I'd like to introduce you to the beautiful Andean under-standing of community, *ayllu* (pronounced "I-You").

Ayllu is the Quechua word for the experience of being intimately connected to one another in our communities, including the land and the whole cosmos. In *ayllu*, we each have our part to play in the well-being of the community, and that value is inherent in both the individual and the greater whole. *Ayllu* honors membership in a community of love and meaning.

My colleagues and I see this principle in action when we travel to rural mountain villages above Peru's Sacred Valley. There, the people mostly live where they were born. They know who they are. They know they belong in and to their families, their communities, their villages, and to the land. For countless generations, their families have stewarded the land, and they continue to actively create relationships with the fertile soil and towering mountains and pristine waters around them, and with each other.

Contrast this with modern Western culture. We emigrated, left our familial and ancestral communities and our birth-places. We're transient, cut off at the roots with each transplanting into a new locale. So how are we to know where we best fit in? We want to experience meaningful belonging, but because we're products of the Western his-story of separation and disconnection from the land, from each other, and from our own hearts, the challenge of belonging is huge.

But where there is support for strengthening and clarifying your gifts, you can take your rightful place in your communities. You get to belong. And you get to follow your big dreams, and to create your life in a way that also benefits your loved ones.

In *ayllu*, everyone contributes to support the community. And the community in turn supports the individual. *Ayllu* is stronger than the sum of all the parts, and it has its own momentum that sustains its members. In an *ayllu* of women—the focus for this chapter—you get to be fully you in community with other women being fully themselves, each offering their innate gifts to the circle. And this creates a magical container for discovery.

In describing *ayllu*, Marti Spiegelman says,

> *"The indigenous understanding of ayllu is that it's the collective's responsibility to support the individual by nurturing, educating, and receiving that person's genius or innate skill, and it's the individual's job to give his or her genius to the collective, all the while receiving the collective's support so the genius is well nourished. No one is left behind or devalued; everyone has a role and a value and meaning on a scale larger than the personal; and everyone benefits."*

We live in a culture that has imposed a false sense of separation on us, a separation that limits our capacity to make a difference, and it's time to recognize that those are artificial limits. Because the world is changing. We're realizing that separation and isolation simply don't work. Looking to nature, it's clear that nothing exists in isolation. From the micro to the macro, everything in nature is connected to and interdependent with its environment. A single Aspen tree lives in the inseparable world of soil, microbes, water, light, insects, the root system of the entire grove. Our bodies reflect this, too. Every cell communicating with other cells, each organ interdependent on the functioning of the rest of the body for health and well-being.

Evolution requires that we wake up to an understanding of community that includes both humans and the land. And the Andean understanding of *ayllu* offers a most compelling and complete model for us to learn from, to find ways to apply in our own culture.

But because we have lived so separate from nature and our own true natures, our work to reclaim our *ayllus* also has to include strengthening a healthy sense of individuality. Not separate from the whole, but intimately connected with the whole. Individuality beyond comparison and competition. This takes work.

It takes work because it takes a lot of unlearning. Most of us did not grow up with the kind of support and visibility that fosters healthy individuality. Most of us either found identities in pleasing others (hyper-sensitive to their needs and shape-shifting our identities in order to meet those needs) or we went the other direction and became overly self-sufficient and autonomous at an early age, perhaps even developing a "me against the world" kind of stance in life. Or we did both, sometimes at the same time.

The bottom line is that a strong, healthy sense of identity is required for healthy *ayllu* participation. In the Andes, that valuable identity formation is more of a given. Here in the West, we have to discover and reclaim our strong sense of identity.

That's why in the ayllus formed through my training program, there's both lots of individual attention and a tending of healthy ayllu dynamics, in alignment with indigenous wisdom. In these groups, women have the chance to explore being in conscious relationship with themselves and others—learning, growing, and evolving every step of the way.

Part of the call from our indigenous teachers for "the Western woman to save the world" includes this: it includes the understanding that participation in our ayllus is *required* to evolve. Such deep experiences of belonging and membership constitute the beginnings of a movement that's already changing the world, as women reclaim the original teachings of wholeness in ayllu with others.

Let's use our heart-knowing, belly-knowing, "intuitive minds" to find resonant communities that will help us grow and thrive, and even flourish. Let's place ourselves into resonant streams of collectivity—in nature and with our tribes—where the seeds of our dreams get nurtured so we all can blossom as we're meant to.

Saying yes

What if we could turn Terry Tempest Williams' observation about our yes's and our no's on its head? Let's transform her observation that:

> *"For far too long we have been seduced into walking a path that did not lead us to ourselves. For far too long we have said yes when we wanted to say no. And for far too long we have said no when we desperately wanted to say yes...."*

into:

> *"We are choosing to walk a path that leads us to ourselves. We are finding the courage to say no when we mean no, and—of vital importance—to say yes when we desperately want to say yes."*

Because it does take a courageous yes to walk in wholeness. It takes a fierce yes to make the commitment search out and join the communities where you can experience the kind of belonging we all long for.

When Lindsey first joined the circle of other women exploring what it's like to walk in wholeness, she often came in with the effects of one or another of her kids clinging to her, crying loudly as they begged her not to leave. They challenged the courageous yes she had chosen to make on her own behalf. She initially felt lost enough in her ayllu, even without that added drama of her children clinging to her. She wondered what in the world she could possibly contribute to the group when she felt so harried and tired, and so disconnected from her dreams, her true nature, even her ability to practice what she was learning. But she kept showing up. She strengthened her commitment to saying yes to her own needs. She insisted on taking time for herself, with other women and in nature, in service of reclaiming her creative life and dreams.

As she did so, Lindsey became more visible. She found her voice and let herself be seen.

A Courageous PATH

Lindsey is reaping the benefits of walking what I call a "Courageous **PATH**." A Courageous PATH is one that will invite your *Courage, Presence, Action, Trust, and Healing.*

Courage. Courage is the voice of your heart saying yes to your dreams. With courage, we learn to respond in the moment to whatever our dreams require for fulfillment, knowing the journey holds rich rewards. The root meanings of the word courage are translated as "heart" and "core." What could be more courageous and full of heart than saying yes to bringing forth the core of who you are and what you have to offer the world!

Presence. Cultivating a sense of solid presence enables your voice and gives you authentic place in your communities. Learning to be solidly present in the here and now, you become able to hold your own while participating in the world. You know where you stand and are able to clearly communicate your position.

Action. A Courageous PATH invites action that stems from your passion, from your dreams. No more skating by with less than you're capable of being and doing. Remember Angeles Arrien's analogy of the oil lamp in Chapter Two? When it comes to realizing your dreams, you can think of the oil as the intuitive well from which you draw your inspiration. The oil is the big dream itself. The flame is your dynamic action in the world. If you have oil with no flame (no action), your dreams will stagnate. If you have only flame separate from the dream, you'll burn out. In fact, the oil and the flame—the dream and concrete action that sources from the dream—are part of one complete process. When your big dreams fuel your actions, you are living authentically, as the author of your own life.

Trust. The work of realizing your dreams requires trust in the dream itself. Your big dreams are resources that inspire you to take action, but you must then also trust your capacity to persevere; the shaping and crafting of meaningful expression is fraught with highs and lows, and there will doubtless be times you question whether you're doing the right thing. Working with mentors who know the territory and have faith in your vision—even when you don't—can be immensely valuable.

Healing. The word "heal" is linguistically related to the word "whole." Healing is vital to releasing the hold the past has on our big dreams. Many of us had childhoods filled with unmet needs, traumas, and demands to be different from how we actually were. The healing process frees energies long held back and reopens the flow of aliveness through the core of our being, thus producing even greater *Courage, Presence, Action, Trust, and Healing.* Healing opens a portal for wholeness.

Eventually, as Lindsey followed a Courageous PATH, the tension in her face and shoulders released. Nervous tics subsided. Comparing photos from a year ago to now, she looks like a different person: more relaxed and alive, soft-ened features, her eyes reflecting deep contact with her heart and soul. Her innate wisdom has re-emerged, and her contributions in her *ayllu* are valued and appreciated by all. She recently shared with the group, "I've participated in lots of women's groups ever since high school. And I'm touched by how loving, supportive, and accepting you all are, the way you all witness me—how *not* common this is in other groups. There's real heart here, and so grounded. When I came to this group, I had been feeling lost and overwhelmed by all the demands in my life. I was so far away from where I am now, and the healthy love in this group has helped me restore my sense of self. Each of us has the intention of being whole, and when we come together in that it's powerful. It's magical. It has changed my life."

Through cultivating a Courageous *PATH*, our hearts open. The dream speaks. With deep listening, the dream itself will reveal each step necessary for its fulfillment and guide us to the places and people that will hold us well.

CHAPTER SIX

Commencement

The Call

To be a visionary is to live life on purpose, to remember your dreams and embody them everyday. That "big something" you feel tugging at your heart? It's your life force with a specific flourish of something special for you to use to create your place in the world. It's your passion—and your passion encodes your life purpose. Our work as visionaries is to empower that passion and purpose in service of fulfilling our biggest dreams and making the difference we're here to make.

For too long we have made our longing to create vibrant, fulfilling lives ride in the passenger seat, window up, glazed eyes on the road. Occasionally, when it gets too damn hot in the car, we'll allow the window down and Creativity herself hangs out wild—wind in her hair, big ol' grin on her face, blissing in a moment of freedom that's far too short-lived.

I don't think this is how human beings are designed. I believe we are creative beings, designed to live in an ongoing, dynamic response and call with Spirit, with Earth, and with all the powers of creation—to live with all our eyes of light wide open, receptive to incoming energies leading us to the fulfillment of our dreams. I believe in our capacity to ride wild waves when the surf's up, excited by the unknown because we have faith in the flow of life.

Overwhelmed and overburdened for too long, with almost super human capacity to nurture others' needs agendas and get things done, we know there's one really important yes we haven't nurtured enough: the one we want to say to our own lives, our own dreams, our special ways of belonging deeply in and to the world.

We are hungry to receive from universal stores of love everything we need to create our lives in wholeness and to teach our children and our grandchildren how to live in wholeness—so that future generations will not get sucked into the vortex of never ending obligation to which many have sacrificed their dreams. Accustomed to moving so fast we can't feel, we're remembering what it's like to pause, to breathe, and to experience life as it unfolds in the moment. We're remembering what it's like to Be. Here. Now. And to take our next steps informed by a love that includes our own selves.

We are the quietly gifted ones who no longer want to hide our gifts from the world. We are the ones steadfastly finding our places to shine, realizing the hidden power at our fingertips to make things happen.

Our wings may have been clipped, but they keep growing back. We rise from the humus that has fertilized our lives to show ourselves again, of earth and of flight. We have been knocking forever at the door of possibility, and now we insist on bursting through. Where we have been wounded, we are healing and mending, once again finding the central core of being in which we come whole. We vow to stand in full presence, full voice—visible to those who dare open their hearts to the truth we carry in our own.

We know that each of us carries a vital message for the world, and our time is now. In love with the world, our feet firmly planted in earth, we are knocking at the door of humanity. Our historic silence may have dampened the fire in our bellies, but we're rekindling it. Our hearts ignite with a passion we've kept too long under wraps, and we are willing to throw lightning bolts back into the places ready to hear us, ready to support us, ready to wake up and mentor our gifts. We are willing to do our inner work so that resources—everything we need to thrive—can start to flow again. We are the ones who say yes to reclaiming wholeness, to restoring our birthright of artfully creating the full-on, full color, wide awake lives of magic and meaning we dream of living *on behalf of humanity*.

We believe in our ability to hear and act in accordance with Spirit, both her whispers and her full-throated arias, as we find our places to shine.

We are the women choosing to walk in wholeness.

APPENDIX A

FEET ON THE GROUND HEALING AND WHOLENESS

Practices for Discovering Your True Nature

We often overlook one of the most accessible sources of help available to us—nature. Nature will always reflect to us our own true nature—if we look for it. Nature is the speech of Spirit, and a powerful medium for connecting with the healing power of Spirit. The following practices are adaptations of indigenous practices I learned from Marti Spiegelman in the Shaman's Light™ Training Program.

Everyday

Notice beauty. When you're out for your daily walk. Driving to work. Shopping for groceries. Wherever you are, make it your practice to notice beauty around you. No matter where you are, so is beauty. Find it and experience it through your senses!

Once a week

Spend an hour outside in nature. There are lots of ways to do this—go for a hike, sit under a tree, walk along the river, find a garden—and be. Just be. It's a great opportunity to notice beauty, too!

When you're challenged

Take the challenge to Pachamama. When facing extreme challenges in life, something transformative happens when you become aware of your feet on the ground. Feeling the ground will help you find your way through. Rather than being taken down by challenge, you can discover a whole new level of presence, a quiet resolve, the loving reminder of Spirit holding you near and dear. You may find yourself invited into a larger conversation of healing and becoming.

Two specific ways to take your challenges to Pachamama are:

1) Lie on the earth, belly down. Imagine opening your belly, or heart, or voice, and give to Pachamama whatever is troubling you. (She knows how to compost it, so if you're someone who might worry about hurting her—don't!) As you release to her, she will send healing energies back to you. Or, another way of saying this, as you release your troubles to Pachamama, you will come into resonance with the deep, slow rhythms of earth that calm and settle our bodies.

2) Go outside. Sit or stand and feel yourself supported by the earth beneath you. Notice what's around you, tuning in

to the sights, sounds, and sensations of being right where you are. As you do this, you'll begin to feel quite present right where you are. Then bring into awareness the challenge you're facing (in other words, feel it!) and ask for a message from nature that helps you meet the challenge. As you ask, begin to watch, listen, or feel for a response in or from nature.

For example, let's say you're working on a project with someone more experienced, and she insists you do things her way. You have some ideas of your own, but are hesitant to speak up for fear of being wrong, or looking foolish, or even just because you're shy. As you bring this challenge into your awareness and ask for nature's help, you might notice a couple of crows squawking. They remind you it's okay to have a voice, even if it sounds funny! Or you notice an unusually shaped tree growing under other trees, but always reaching for the best sources of light available. It gives you the courage to be exactly who you are and ask for help when you need it, without worrying about what anyone else may think.

Whenever you can

Take advantage of every opportunity to tune in to the gifts Pachamama offers—food, shelter, beauty, 'scent-sations', your birth into this world. Send your love to her, kiss the ground, and make an offering to her. Gather her love for you up through the soles of your feet and into your heart.

Then say a prayer for our world and let's walk on together toward our biggest dreams—hand in hand, heart to heart— as Pachamama's children, today and always. Your participation really does make a difference on every level, from your personal life to the planetary and beyond.

ACKNOWLEDGEMENTS

Writing a book is very much a collective project. I am celebrating the following people, whose contributions have been invaluable in stewarding this book to life!

I couldn't be more grateful to the women and men willing to explore this special knowledge of wholeness with me. Your stories are interwoven here, and you're the real reason I wrote *Walking in Wholeness*. What comes through on these pages is because you are willing to show up and participate in the conversation.

Marti Spiegelman has mentored my awakenings in wholeness, no doubt in ways I haven't even been able to see yet. What she offers is truly a pearl beyond price! And her assistance with keeping my references true to their original sources helped to ensure the integrity of this project. Marti is the leader of the Shamans Light™ tribe I get to adventure with into all kinds of stunning landscapes of earth and consciousness. I'm especially thankful for my ayllu sister Ellen Bachmeyer's vision, availability, and alliance during the writing of this book.

Huge thanks go to Peter Tsantilis whose encouragement and belief in my capacity for this work inspires me every day.

Angela Lauria and The Author Incubator team must have some very special elixir for nurturing difference-making books into existence—and authors into leaders. Angela intuitively redirected my focus for this book about halfway through the process, and it made all the difference between struggling to finish and writing with joy. Kate Makled's attuned presence and insightful developmental support and editing have my deepest respect and appreciation. Special thanks go to Kelly Pratt and Heidi Miller, too, for their patience and open-hearted assistance with landing the beautiful cover design that graces this book.

My husband, Jim, once again sacrificed our precious time together, supportively witnessing every celebration and crisis of faith, and contributing keen editorial insight that caught more than a few mixed metaphors and unintended hidden meanings. Mwah!

I bow, too, to the community of extraordinary indigenous teachers, Santa Tierras, ancestors, angelic presences, muses, and other bringers of light who spark my best writing and my passion for helping to restore the world to wholeness.

ABOUT THE AUTHOR

Kimberlie Chenoweth is the founder of *The Wholeness Project*™ and developer of a transformational mentoring program that helps people claim their place in the world and create the life they're meant to be living, in wholeness. She specializes in helping women bring their authentic essence to light so they can find their places of true belonging and *thrive*. These sensitive, insightful women often identify as healers, teachers, artists, and leaders who long for fulfillment and meaning at home, work, and play.

The author of the Amazon bestselling book, *Reclaiming Wholeness*, Kimberlie has a Master's degree in Counseling, and is a certified Master NLP Practitioner and endorsed member of the Core Transformation Trainers Association.

She enjoyed 22 years in private practice as a psychotherapist and personal development trainer before launching *The Wholeness Project*™ in 2012. She grew up exploring a world of metaphysics and mysticism, and has studied traditions of the East, West and native Americas. She has sat in silence, traveled widely, and committed to a process of deep healing and transformation over many years. She is initiated as an Andean mesa carrier and wisdom keeper.

Kimberlie is a natural at getting to the core of things—your uniqueness, your potential, and the stuff that gets in the way of you being all that you can be. She lives in rural Western Colorado with her husband, two dogs, beautiful sunsets, and tantalizing hiking trails. She rarely leaves the house without her camera.

If the knowledge shared in this book excites, intrigues, or otherwise resonates for you, please visit Kimberlie's website at www.TheWholenessProject.com. If you'd like to talk with her, you're welcome to schedule a complimentary discovery session at www.kimberlie.acuityscheduling.com.

difference press

Difference Press offers solopreneurs, including life coaches, healers, consultants, and community leaders, a comprehensive solution to get their books written, published, and promoted. A boutique-style alternative to self-publishing, Difference Press boasts a fair and easy-to-understand profit structure, low-priced author copies, and author-friendly contract terms. Its founder, Dr. Angela Lauria, has been bringing to life the literary ventures of hundreds of authors-in-transformation since 1994.

LET'S START A MOVEMENT WITH YOUR MESSAGE
You've seen other people make a difference with a book. Now it's your turn. If you are ready to stop watching and start taking massive action. Reach out.

"Yes, I'm ready!"

In a market where hundreds of thousands books are published every year and are never heard from again, all participants of The Author Incubator have bestsellers that are actively changing lives and making a difference.

In less than two years we've created over 100 bestselling books in a row, 90% from first-time authors. As a result, our regular book programs are selling out in advance and we are selecting only the highest quality and highest potential applicants for our future programs.

Our program doesn't just teach you how to write a book—our team of coaches, developmental editors, copy editors, art directors, and marketing experts incubate you from book idea to published bestseller, ensuring that the book you create can actually make a difference in the world. We only work with the people who will use their book to get out there and make that difference.

If you have life-or world-changing ideas or services, a servant's heart, and the willingness to do what it REALLY takes to make a difference in the world with your book, go to http://theAuthorIncubator.com/ apply to complete an application for the program today.

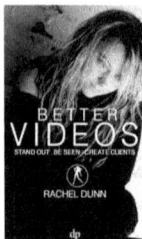

Better Videos: Stand out. Be Seen. Create Clients.

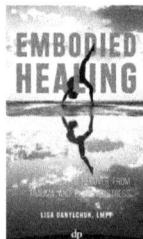

by Rachel Dunn

Embodied Healing: Using Yoga to Recover from Trauma and Extreme Stress

by Lisa Danylchuk

Evolve Your Life: Rethink Your Biggest Picture Through Conscious Evolution

by Sheila Cash

Growing Your Separate Ways: 8 Straight Steps to Separating with the Same Intention of Love and Respect You Had...

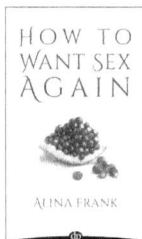

by Leah Ruppel

How to Want Sex Again: Rekindling Passion with EFT

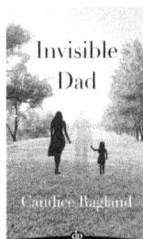

by Alina Frank

Invisible Dad: How to Heal as a Fatherless Daughter

by Candice Ragland

Not Your Average 5K: A Practical 8-Week Training Plan for Beginning Runners

by Jill Angie

The Cancer Whisperer: How to Let Cancer Heal Your Life

by Sophie Sabbage

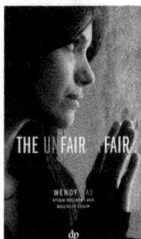

The Unfair Affair: How to Strengthen and Save Your Marriage, or Move on with Confidence, After Infidelity

by Wendy Kay

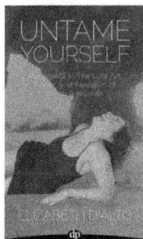

Untame Yourself: Reconnect to the Lost Art, Power and Freedom of Being a Woman

by Elizabeth DiAlto

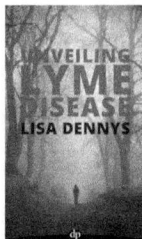

Unveiling Lyme Disease: Is This What's Behind Your Chronic Illness?

by Lisa Dennys

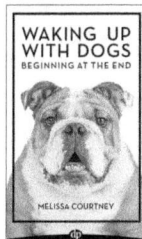

Waking Up With Dogs: Beginning at the End

by Melissa Courtney

Whoops! I Forgot To Achieve My Potential: Create Your Very Own Personal Change Management Strategy to Get the...

by Maggie Huffman

Personal Finance That Doesn't Suck: A 5-step Guide to Quit Budgeting, Start Wealth Building and Get the Most from...

by Mindy Crary

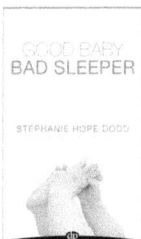

Good Baby, Bad Sleeper: Discover Your Child's Sleep Personality To Finally Get the Sleep You Need

by Stephanie Hope Dodd

How You Can Be with His ADHD: What You Can Do To Rescue Your Relationship When Your Partner Has Adult ADHD

by Mark Julian